Susan Scott Cesaritti
Maria Merlini   Barbara Tavolari

# THE MUSEO DELL'OPERA
## Siena

Introductory texts by
Senio Bruschelli, Enzo Carli, Bruno Santi

SCALA

# CONTENTS

3 Foreword
7 Preface
11 Introduction
14 Sala della "Madonna dagli Occhi Grossi"
26 Sala dei Conversari or dell'Alfieri
36 Sala degli Arazzi
40 Panorama from the "Facciatone"
41 Sala del Tesoro
50 Sala di Duccio
64 Sala di Jacopo della Quercia
65 Sala del Crocifisso
68 Sala dei Cartoni
70 Galleria delle Statue
76 Sala del Portone Centrale del Duomo
76 Sala degli Apostoli
78 Church of San Niccolò in Sasso

© 1998 SCALA Group S.p.A., Florence

Photographic acknowledgements: SCALA ARCHIVE (M. Sarri), except for p. 16 (Archivio fotografico della Soprintendenza per i Beni Artistici e Storici di Siena) and p. 75 (Opera della Metropolitana, F. Lensini).

Translation: Susan Scott Cesaritti
Editing: Marilena Vecchi
Printed by: "Arti Grafiche" Stampa Nazionale, Calenzano (Florence), 2002

Back cover: Duccio di Buoninsegna, *The Funeral of the Virgin* (Maestà: Front upper register)

# FOREWORD

The Museo dell'Opera (the Museum of the Cathedral Vestry Board) was established officially in 1869, when the Prefect of Siena informed the Rector of the Opera that the plan to create a museum within the ambit of the Opera had been approved by the Ministry of Public Education, the government agency responsible at that time for museums and monuments.

It was a time of great fervor in the accomplishment of ambitious projects. In Florence, ten years earlier, the Museo Nazionale del Bargello had been created, and in 1860 the Galleria d'Arte Moderna opened its doors. In 1882 the Pinacoteca di Brera in Milan would open, and in 1889 the Galleria Nazionale would be established in Rome.

Once he had the Ministry's approval, Ferdinando Rubini, Rector of the Opera, made concrete moves to realize a museum with a broad range of exhibits, displaying not only art works and objects originally in the cathedral, but also illuminated manuscripts and sacred objects and decorations from suppressed convents, as well as works of art, many of them of great value, which as styles and taste changed had been moved from their original destinations, especially from the XIIIth century on. He was also given permission to expand the museum's premises by repurchasing in 1874 from the provincial administration some of the buildings, including the panoramic facade of the unfinished new cathedral, contiguous to the space created at the end of the XIVth century by bricking in the first three bays of the right nave of the new cathedral.

The undertaking begun by Rubini at the end of the 1860s continued uninterrupted over time. Giuseppe Partini, architect of the Opera after 1867, created the Galleria delle Statue, still in use today as choice exhibition space for an important collection of Sienese XIVth century sculpture.

In 1875 Francesco Brogi compiled the catalogue of the antique sculpture collection, and in 1882 Carlo and Emanuele Santi collaborated to prepare a general catalogue of the museum.

Acquisitions continued over the years, and in 1875 the Rector of the Opera communicated to the Ministry of Public Education the results obtained in the collection of "antique art objects" coming also from churches in the province, describing his intention to strengthen the museum's holdings.

Acquisitions worthy of special mention are the marble sculpture of the sleeping child, entitled *The Sleep of Innocence*, which Laudomia Bichi Ruspoli Forteguerri donated to the museum in 1953, and the incorporation in 1996 of the church of San Niccolò in Sasso into the museum complex. Rubini's activity was thus followed by that of other rectors succeeding to the post of head of the Opera, who continued to acquire works and to create display space that today place the Museo dell'Opera in the avant-garde among private museums.

The visitor, following the suggested itinerary, can admire a series of works illustrating the periods of Sienese painting from the Byzantine era of Guido da Siena to the magnificent Mannerism of Domenico Beccafumi.

Crossing the Sala degli Arazzi, resplendent in the compositional and chromatic richness of its sublime specimens of embroidery with gold and silk, one can climb to the top of the unfinished facade of the new cathedral, called the "Facciatone" (big facade), overlooking the city: an almost continuous stretch of roofs practically overlapping each other, broken only by domes and belltowers, in a harmony created by the play of volumes and the fusion between the built environment of the city and the wedges of green trees and spaces inserted into the architectonic texture.

But the museum is not only a display of great art works, it is also a forge for cultural interests which come to fruition in the activities connected with the historical archives, the library, and a series of manifestations and initiatives to bring the public close to the art, to foster culture, and to stimulate creative energy. The generous activity of the Friends of the Museum permits a program of exhibitions, lectures, and initiatives of various kinds which also have an important economic impact, especially considering that the Opera della Metropolitana finances its general operations and maintenance solely with the income generated by entrance fees. Grand special projects require financing from public and private sources, whose availability depends on the efficient management of the museum and on its ability to satisfy what is by now an international public.

At the museum's exit is a display of reproductions in gold and silver of masterpieces of great artists of the past, offered for sale, in line with initiatives already successfully undertaken by the world's great museums. These objects are created by leading craftsmen, whose superior skill guarantees a perfect reproduction of the original art work, satisfying the desire of visitors to remember the beauty they have seen by taking away with them a tangible sign of it.

The purpose of this guide is to offer a succinct instrument for visiting the museum, by giving information essential for identifying the work of art, its author and subject, and some brief notes about its importance in cultural history. Inclusion of the inventory number enables the visitor to request from the museum administration further details and photographs, and thus to participate in the life of the museum, which is a living entity and not simply the collection and display of objects from the past.

In presenting this guide, I cannot refrain from thanking the publishers who made its production possible and the three art historians who carried out the onerous task of creating an inventory and catalogue of the works in the museum. It is our hope that this effort will represent the first step toward preparation of a general catalogue on a scholarly level.

*Senio Bruschelli*
Rector of the Opera della Metropolitana

Miniature representing Siena from the Book of Census Records.
Siena, Archivio di Stato, *Biccherna* 746

# PREFACE

The Museo dell'Opera, even more than the Pinacoteca Nazionale (at that time Regia) whose direction Superintendent Peleo Bacci entrusted to me when I came to Siena in 1939, is the one I love and admire most. I used to go there almost every day, fascinated as a Pisan by its exceptional collection of sculptures and like everyone by that incomparable masterpiece which is Duccio's *Maestà*.

In the museum, through the benevolence and trust of my predecessors as Rector, among whom it gives me special pleasure to remember Ezio Cantagalli, I enjoyed the greatest freedom of access, as though I were already its director. Between the end of 1940 and the beginning of 1941 the transfer, already providentially begun at the end of the XIXth century, continued of Giovanni Pisano's astounding statues, among them *Miriam*, from the cathedral facade, thus affording me the occasion of publishing in 1941 a volume, *Sculture del Duomo di Siena* (Einaudi), which illustrated some of the works displayed in the museum. In 1946 the first guide to the museum was published by Ticci in Siena, giving a fairly extensive historical and critical treatment to all of the museum's holdings. Since that time, the museum has undergone significant changes and growth. As an example, at the center of the Galleria delle Statue on the ground floor once stood the famous marble group of the *Three Graces*, the very fine Roman copy of a Greek original from the Hellenistic period, with its beautiful base carved by Antonio Federighi, which after numerous wanderings was returned in 1976, thanks to the enlightened understanding of the archbishop, Msgr. Mario Jsmaele Castellano, to the Piccolomini Library in the cathedral, to which it was originally destined after its purchase in Rome by Cardinal Francesco Piccolomini, later Pope Pius III. In that same year, its place in the gallery was filled by Jacopo della Quercia's last work (1438), earlier in the now destroyed chapel of Saint Sebastian in the cathedral, a large relief purchased by the Italian state from the heirs of the well-known journalist and critic Ugo Ojetti, destining it to the Museo Nazionale del Bargello in Florence but consenting to its deposit in our museum, thus returning it to the "workshop" in which it was sculpted. Another

Pinturicchio, *Enea Silvio Piccolomini, Bishop of Siena, Presides over the Meeting of Frederick III and Eleanor of Aragon*, detail showing the Cathedral and the unfinished facade of the Duomo Nuovo. Siena, Piccolomini Library

major accession in this same gallery was accomplished in 1985 with the tondo of the *Virgin of Pardon*, executed by Donatello toward 1457 for the old altar of Saint Callistus in the cathedral and in 1675-1677 transferred to the lunette above the side door of the Duomo (now substituted by a copy); another tondo of the *Virgin and Child*, earlier placed at the top of Urbano da Cortona's facade for the old chapel of the Virgin of Grace (later the chapel of Votive Offerings), was purchased in 1983 by Monte dei Paschi bank and donated to the Opera del Duomo. A radical change in the arrangement of the rooms was carried out in 1969-1971 with the complete transformation, under the direction of the architect Minissi, of the large hall on the first floor, equipped with climate control equipment for the conservation of the great painted complex of the *Maestà* by Duccio, which earlier had been installed in a room on the second floor that was too sensitive to changes in temperature. Along with the *Maestà*, the room holds Duccio's delicate and precious panel of the *Madonna of Crevole* and the triptych of the *Birth of the Virgin* by Pietro Lorenzetti.

The room on the second floor, whose insulation was in the meantime significantly improved, became the display space for the *Madonna of the Vow of Montaperti* (a title which suits it much better than that of *Virgin of the Big Eyes*), and around it on the walls were placed important works including the doors of the *Relic Cupboard* by Benedetto di Bindo, reunited with their predellas, a polyptych of 1423 by Gregorio di Cecco di Luca, four panels of a polyptych by Ambrogio Lorenzetti, a *Saint Jerome* and a predella panel by Giovanni di Paolo and other panels attributed to him, to the Master of Città di Castello, to Taddeo di Bartolo, Sassetta, and other Sienese painters of the XIVth and XVth centuries, while from the room destined to become the Duccio room the large altarpiece of the *Baptism of Christ* by the Brescianini (1524) was moved to the Galleria delle Statue and installed inside a monumental altar complex dated 1683, and Beccafumi's *Saint Paul* was taken to the room named for Alfieri.

After 1946, an important addition to the museum's holdings came from the suppressed Company of San Giovanni Battista della Morte, whose headquarters was part of the museum building, which yielded the wooden sculpture of *Saint John the Baptist*, recognized by me without doubt in 1949 as Francesco di Giorgio Martini's first work, commissioned in 1464 and at some point ending up in the parish church of Fogliano, and the four catafalque headboards painted by Sodoma and highly praised by Vasari. In the second half of the 1970s five gilded wooden statues by Jacopo della Quercia and his workshop were moved from the church of San Martino into a small room dedicated just to them, while in the room now called Sala del Crocifisso the documents which had been taken out of it during the war and that nonetheless still were included in the 1946 guide were not put back in place, because they were considered to be difficult to read and of interest only to specialists. They were instead put in the Archives of the Opera del Duomo and later entrusted to the careful skill of Prof. Stefano Moscadelli, who published in Munich in 1995, under the auspices of the Kunsthistorisches Institut in Florence, a complete, scholarly inventory of them. The return of the documents to the Archives, whose Reading Room was made more comfortable, permitted a more rational arrangement of the splendid collection of illuminated manuscripts, while other changes in display space were made in the Sala del Tesoro, enriched with the magnificent XVIIIth century *Reliquary of Saint Clement* and the panel of the *Virgin of Humility* by Paolo di Giovanni Fei, both coming into the museum from the cathedral, and in the large room historically named for Alfieri and whose title "Sala dei Conversari" or Conversation Room I refuse to recognize (because in museums one does not converse, but one admires and studies, preferably in silence).

This was the situation of the museum described in a guide published in 1989 on the occasion of the donation to the museum by the Saint-Gobain company of the protective vandal-proof glass placed in front of the *Maestà* and other works in the same room. Since the 1989 guide, other works have entered the museum, including Sano di Pietro's large panels of *Saint Bernardine* and of *The Saint preaching in the Campo* and *in Piazza San Francesco*, earlier in the chapter room of the cathedral and placed here on loan, Giovanni di Paolo's *Saint John and the Virgin Mourning at the Foot of the Cross*, now displayed on either side of the wooden *Crucifix* by Giovanni Pisano but earlier in the oratory of SS. Giovannino e Gennaro, under the jurisdiction of the Opera, from which was also transferred the large standard painted on both sides by Rustichino (ca. 1621) and Rutilio and Domenico Manetti.

In 1989-1990, with the display elsewhere of the drawings and illuminated manuscripts, in the room following that of Jacopo della Quercia was recomposed the group of wooden statues from the chapel of Ser Galgano di Cerbone, also called "Chapel of the Crucifix" and the only one which has survived intact, placing to the sides of the XIVth century *Crucifix* called "of the Widows," which was earlier in the cathedral sacristy, the two wooden statues of the *Mourning Virgin and Saint John the Evangelist* carved in 1414 by Domenico di Niccolò dei Cori, which after many vicissitudes and after restoration in 1987 had ended up in the church of San Pietro a Ovile. It is my hope that the *Lamentation over the Dead Christ* (1421) by Alberto di Betto da Assisi, now under the small altar in the facade of the Piccolomini Library, will be placed under this group and substituted in the cathedral by a copy. Nonetheless, the story of the museum is not made up only of transfers and new accessions. Two works mentioned in the 1946 guide are no longer there. One is a mediocre small panel (47x34 cm), which disappeared inexplicably in September 1968; I was able to give a name to its author, who in the guide is called "Pseudo Ambrogio di Baldese," but in reality is Ventura di Moro, a modest Florentine painter active in the territory of Siena in the early decades of the XVth century. The other is the very fine polychrome terracotta statue of *The Kneeling Saint John the Evangelist*, which in response to various requests and promises was sent in 1987 to the Basilica dell'Osservanza so that it could be reunited with Giacomo Cozzarelli's large composition of the *Lamentation over the Dead Christ*, to which it certainly originally belonged.

The last part of my long period as Rector saw two significant enlargements of the museum itinerary. One was the transformation of two storerooms adjacent to the Galleria delle Statue on the ground floor into display space for the sections of the columns carved by Giovanni Pisano and his assistants for the main portal of the Duomo, followed by a larger room where the large statues of *Apostles* by the school of Giovanni Pisano, removed from the eaves of the cathedral roof (not their original location), prepare the visitor for the marvelous group of the *Blessing Redeemer adored by Two Angels*, the work of Giovanni d'Agostino (ca. 1345-46) and the last masterpiece of the great Sienese sculptural tradition of the XIVth century, removed from the outer lunette of the side door of the new cathedral and substituted by a copy. The second innovation was the annexation to the museum, connected by an inner staircase designed by the architect Mario Rodolfo Terrosi, of the church of San Niccolò in Sasso, which had been closed to the public for a number of years. The small church is a veritable treasure chest of paintings, stucco decorations, frescoes, and sculptures of the early XVIIth century, whose great and unique artistic and historical value is practically unknown to the Sienese themselves.

Completion of both these projects, the two new sculpture rooms and the church of San Niccolò, inaugurated on 9 September 1995, is the merit of the new Rector of the Opera, Senio Bruschelli, who is also responsible for the initiative of the publication of this brief guide, to which I wish the very best of success.

*Enzo Carli*
Honorary Rector of the Opera della Metropolitana
Director of the Museum

# INTRODUCTION

The complex history of the construction and decoration of the Duomo of Siena, rightly one of the most celebrated and admired cathedrals in Italy, is visible not only in the building's exterior and interior. The building is unique in its possession of stylistic characteristics of the architecture from beyond the Alps, as though to seal in marble and stone the relationships which for so long characterized the cultural and political exchange between Siena and France, and to whose numerous connections art history is a witness. The passage of so many centuries, with various phases of remodeling, changes in taste, renovations, completions and additions, have all left numerous, significant traces not only in its architectural aspect but also in the myriad objects inside the church.

Thus whoever, moved by curiosity or by a desire to know the whole story, wishes to follow the course of these events (to the degree that this is possible with an institution which has to deal with the irreparable loss of great treasures from the most important church in Siena – just to cite two among many: Simone Martini's *Annunciation*, now in the Uffizi, and the *Virgin of the Snow*, in the Contini Bonacossi collection, also in Florence) must turn to the Museo dell'Opera della Metropolitana di Siena, not only the host of a dizzying vantage point for a panoramic view of the city because of the presence inside its walls of the monumental facade of the new cathedral – this too a valuable documentation of the project of enlarging and renovating the church – but also an anthology of the highest documentary value of all the changes that took place in the decoration of the Duomo's interior.

Inside its walls are the original statues from its facade and sides, a crowd of marble figures springing forth from the workshop of Giovanni Pisano, now substituted by copies to prevent their ultimate, definitive destruction; portions of the amazing polychrome floor; altarpieces from the XVth, XVth and XVIIth centuries created by Siena's leading painters and sculptors in each epoch: Sano di Pietro, Matteo di Giovanni, Domenico Beccafumi, Genga, Jacopo della Quercia, Domenico di Niccolò "dei Cori," Valdambrino. Then there are the precious works in gold and silver and precious stones, including the very rich treasury of the chapel of the Virgin of Votive Offerings, donated by the Chigi family. These are – very briefly – some of the names of the most important artists and works present in the museum. To these must be added altar hangings, liturgical vestments, sacred objects – everything that was needed for celebration of the liturgy in Siena Cathedral and that changes in taste and in ritual had caused to be replaced over time. And finally the emblematic painting of Sienese figurative culture, Duccio's *Maestà*, to which an entire room is devoted. In a dimmed and silent atmosphere, with its extraordinary chromatic richness and imaginative figurative solutions it can still evoke the joy of a festive people as they accompanied the great work from the painter's workshop to its destination on the high altar of the city's major church.

The fitting complement to a visit to the cathedral and its many examples of the creativity stimulated by a community which found embodied there its religious feeling and its civic pride, the Museo dell'Opera del Duomo is one of the places where the persistence is palpable of a culture which continues to be aware that it has contributed in an essential way to the establishment of Western art and has made an effort to present – to the degree possible given the flow of historical events – its living memory.

*Bruno Santi*
Superintendent for the Historical and Artistic Patrimony
of the Provinces of Siena and Grosseto

Rutilio Manetti, city map of Siena (1609-10), detail including the Cathedral and the "Facciatone". Siena, Archivio di Stato

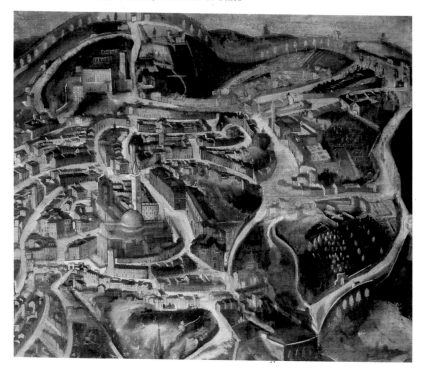

# The Museo dell'Opera

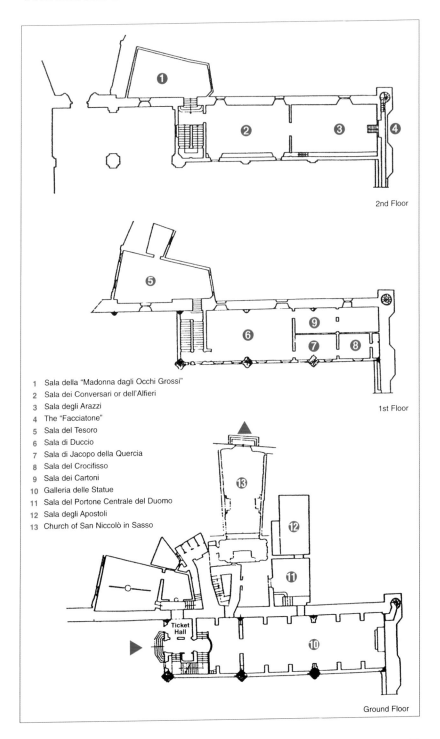

2nd Floor

1st Floor

1  Sala della "Madonna dagli Occhi Grossi"
2  Sala dei Conversari or dell'Alfieri
3  Sala degli Arazzi
4  The "Facciatone"
5  Sala del Tesoro
6  Sala di Duccio
7  Sala di Jacopo della Quercia
8  Sala del Crocifisso
9  Sala dei Cartoni
10  Galleria delle Statue
11  Sala del Portone Centrale del Duomo
12  Sala degli Apostoli
13  Church of San Niccolò in Sasso

Ticket Hall

Ground Floor

13

# Sala della "Madonna dagli Occhi Grossi"

This room takes its name from the XIIIth century panel of the Sienese school called *The Virgin with Big Eyes*. The image was placed on the high altar of the cathedral when, on the eve of the battle of Montaperti fought on 4 September 1260, the Sienese people led by Bonagiunta Lucari and Provenzano Salvani dedicated the city to the Virgin Mary in exchange for her protection; after bloody combat, the battle was won by the Sienese. The room contains valuable examples of Sienese painting from the early XIIIth century to well into the XVIth century, represented by the four catafalque headboards by Sodoma. The XVth century panels attributed to Taddeo di Bartolo are the first representation of the articles of the "Creed" in Sienese art, a theme that is peculiar to this territory

and can be seen elsewhere in the city in the vaults of the Baptistery frescoed by Vecchietta and in the choir stalls of the chapel inside Palazzo Pubblico by Domenico di Niccolò. Important works by Giovanni di Paolo and Riccio, among others, complete the room's offerings.

A M B R O G I O   L O R E N Z E T T I   (Siena, doc. from 1319 to 1348)
**Saint Catherine of Alexandria; Saint Benedict; Saint Francis of Assisi;
Saint Mary Magdalene**
121x43 cm (each), tempera on wood; inv. 3501

These are four panels of a polyptych which may have had a *Virgin and Child* as its center, painted for the cathedral around the third decade of the XIVth century. They are usually assigned to the young Ambrogio Lorenzetti.

G I O V A N N I   A N T O N I O   B A Z Z I   called  S O D O M A
(Vercelli 1477 - Siena 1549)
**Saint John the Baptist; Virgin and Child; The Dead Jesus;
Saint Bernardine of Siena**
63x42 cm (each), oil on wood; inv. 3504, 3505, 3509, 3510

Sodoma was one of the Sienese painters most in demand in the early
decades of the XVIth century. He painted these four catafalque headboards
between 1526 and 1527 for the Company of San Giovanni della Morte.
Of very high quality, these images are distinguished by the serene dignity of
the figures, seen especially in the suffering Christ, and the calm, slightly
Raphaelesque sweetness of the Virgin and Child.

S A N O   D I   P I E T R O   (Siena 1405 - 1481)
**Saint Bernardine Preaching in Piazza del Campo; Saint Bernardine
of Siena; Saint Bernardine Preaching in Piazza San Francesco**
163x102 cm (side panels); 218x100 (central panel), tempera on wood;
inv. 3506, 3507, 3508

Painted around 1440, these panels are important not only because of their very high quality compared with much of the production of this prolific painter, but also as historical documents. In fact, Sano di Pietro certainly saw Saint Bernardine, one of the most popular preachers who ever lived, while he was still alive, and the image reproduced here can be considered a portrait from life. The preacher died in 1444 and by 1450 had already been canonized. Of the numerous images of Saint Bernardine painted by Sano di Pietro, especially after the saint's death, this is one of the finest both for the handling of the paint and for its practically perfect condition; the beautiful gilded frame was made in the XIXth century. The saint is holding Christ's monogram, which he designed after a vision; this was the object of such veneration that the administrators of the Sienese republic had it placed on the facade of Palazzo Pubblico, where it can still be seen. The smaller panels represent two moments in the cycle of sermons preached by Saint Bernardine in Siena in 1425, in the square in front of the church of San Francesco, and in 1427 in Piazza del Campo. The paintings offer important documentary evidence of the still unfinished facade of the church of San Francesco and Palazzo Pubblico as they appeared in those years.

BENEDETTO DI BINDO (Siena, doc. from 1411 to 1417)
and assistants
**Reliquary cabinet**
recto: *Sixteen Angels*; verso: *Stories of the Legend of the True Cross*; predellas:
*Two Angels and Four Prophets*; *Three Angels and Three Prophets*
136x95.5 cm (each door); 52x175 cm (each predella), tempera on wood;
inv. 3511, 3518

These are the doors, painted on both sides, of the cabinet holding relics in
the chapel of the cathedral sacristy. On the exterior, half-figures of angels
hold cartouches indicating the relics stored in their respective compartments.
On the inside of the doors are stories of the True Cross, a piece of which was
venerated in the Duomo. An important example of Sienese craftsmanship in
the XVth century, the cabinet was made by the celebrated sculptor
Domenico di Niccolò dei Cori, author of the beautiful choir stalls in the
chapel inside Palazzo Pubblico, and the painted decoration was entrusted to
Benedetto di Bindo, who carried it out with assistants around 1412.

STEFANO DI GIOVANNI called SASSETTA
(Cortona? end of XIVth century - Siena 1450)
**Virgin of Humility**
66x44 cm, tempera on wood; inv. 3512

The image of the Virgin seated on the ground as a sign of her humility, often nursing the Child (see also no. 3514 in this room), comes from a lost prototype by Simone Martini which was widely imitated in the XIVth and XVth centuries. This painting, from around 1435, even though badly damaged by past overcleaning, is a lovely example of the linear and chromatic grace of XVth century Sienese art combined with a solid sense of volume manifested in the Child, showing Sassetta's evident contact with Florence and particularly the art of Masaccio.

GREGORIO DI CECCO (Siena, doc. from 1389 to 1423)
**Virgin of Humility with Angels and Saints**
137x82 cm, tempera on wood; inv. 3514

Signed and dated 1423, this is a fine example, even though incomplete, of a XVth century polyptych. In the central panel, the Virgin nurses her Child surrounded by musical angels and surmounted by the dove of the Holy Spirit. The side panels hold images of Saints Augustine, John the Baptist, Peter, and Paul; in the side pinnacles appear Saints Blaise and Ansanus, and in the central one the Assumption of the Virgin Mary. The only certain work by this painter, who was the student and adoptive son of Taddeo di Bartolo (whose *Articles of the Creed* are in this room), the painting repeats elements from XIVth century art in its attention to decorative detail and the gold striations in the Virgin's cloak, rendered here with Gothic elegance and grace.

MASTER OF OVILE (BARTOLOMEO BULGARINI?) (doc. in Siena and Florence from 1337 to 1378)
**Virgin and Child**
92x58 cm, tempera on wood; inv. 3517

This is the work of a master earlier called conventionally "Master of Ovile" or "Ugolino Lorenzetti" and now generally recognized as Bartolomeo Bulgarini, who died in 1378. The faces of the Mother and Child clearly show their derivation from prototypes by Pietro Lorenzetti, here combined with influences from the art of Simone Martini in the linear development of the drapery.

Attrib. to the MASTER OF TRESSA
(Siena, first half of the XIIIth century)
**Madonna dagli Occhi Grossi**
97x67 cm, tempera on wood; inv. 3522

The oldest surviving image of the Virgin in Sienese art, this panel, called
*The Virgin with Big Eyes*, was probably the central section of an altarpiece
placed on the high altar of the cathedral. It unites Romanesque elements
like the monumental figure inserted solidly into its surrounding space with
Byzantine aspects like the severe frontality of the Virgin and a pronounced
decorative sense which give the painting the appearance of an icon. It shares
stylistic traits with an altar dossal in the Pinacoteca in Siena, dated 1215,
also attributed to the anonymous Master of Tressa, but perhaps it should be
assigned to a slightly later period, toward the third decade of the Duecento.

## SALA DEI CONVERSARI OR DELL'ALFIERI

The "Conversation" or Alfieri Room (Vittorio Alfieri read some of his plays in this room in 1777) corresponds with the highest point of the right nave of the new cathedral and contains important paintings, true jewels of Sienese art between the second half of the XVth and the first half of the XVIth century. But before entering the room, along the wall above the last flight of stairs one can admire some fragments of frescoes by Riccio. These paintings, now detached and mounted on cardboard, were above the altar of the Four Crowned Saints in the Duomo, destroyed at the beginning of the XVIIth century when Cardinal Flavio Chigi renovated all of the altars in the church. In this work, painted around 1534-1535, Riccio gives evidence of the neo-Raphaelesque influence of Baldassare Peruzzi, who in this period was architect of the Opera del Duomo.

Entering now the Alfieri Room, on the left wall are two altarpieces by Matteo di Giovanni, the *Virgin and Child with Four Saints* and the *Virgin and Child with Saints Anthony of Padua and Bernardine*. Both have been recently restored, the first in December 1996, the second for the Francesco di Giorgio exhibition in 1993.

In the center of the room are displayed two XVIIth century paintings: *The Baptism of Christ* by Francesco Rustici, and *Saint John the Baptist Preaching* by Rutilio Manetti, who infused new life into Sienese painting of the XVIIth century, to the point of being considered, because of his faithful adherence to reality, a Caravaggesque artist.

The room also houses an extraordinary example of Sienese Mannerist painting: Domenico Beccafumi offers evidence of his mastery in the large panel of *Saint Paul Enthroned*. Works by Luca Giordano, Pomarancio (an altarpiece commissioned for one of the altars in the cathedral), and Girolamo Genga complete the brief but exceptional panorama of art in the room.

Finally, on display are a series of altar hangings of precious fabrics embroidered with silk from the XVth to the XVIIIth centuries.

MATTEO DI GIOVANNI
(Borgo San Sepolcro 1430 - Siena 1497)
**Virgin and Child Enthroned with Two Angels and Saints John
the Evangelist, Nicholas of Bari, Gregory, and Jerome**
predella: *The Martyrdom of Saint John the Evangelist; Saint Nicholas Provides
a Dowry for Three Girls; The Resurrection of Christ; Saint Gregory Leads the
Cardinals in Procession during the Plague in Rome; Saint Jerome Removes a
Thorn from the Lion's Paw;* on the ends: Celsi family coats of arms
241x188 cm; 294x39 cm, tempera on wood; inv. 3001

This altarpiece with a five-panel predella (today recently restored to its
original splendor) was commissioned by the Celsi family for the Saint
Nicholas altar in the Duomo (the second on the right nave wall).
The work, painted in 1480, reflects the idiom of the artist's maturity;
although influenced by the styles of Florence, Umbria, and Padua (due to
his encounter with Liberale da Verona and Girolamo da Cremona, who
were illuminating manuscripts for Siena Cathedral during this period), he
remained firmly anchored in the Sienese tradition. The result is a work of
great charm, especially in the gentle, melancholy figure of the Virgin under
the marble arch of her throne, in contrast with the solemn monumentality
of the four saints to her sides.

M A T T E O   D I   G I O V A N N I
(Borgo San Sepolcro 1430 - Siena 1497)
**Virgin and Child with Saints Anthony of Padua and Bernardine and Angels**
254x180 cm, tempera on wood; inv. 3003

On the frame at the bottom: OPUS MATHEI IOHANNI MCCCCLX. The panel, which originally had a predella, now lost, with figures of the twelve apostles, was painted in 1460 for the altar of Saint Anthony of Padua in the Baptistery of Siena, and is considered Matteo di Giovanni's masterpiece. Recent studies have emphasized the close connection between this Sienese artist and Piero della Francesca (especially with regard to *The Baptism of Christ* in the National Gallery in London, for which Matteo painted several parts). Rays of light flood the entire panel, setting up a vibration of the extraordinary chromatic range in the saints' clothing and the wings of the angels. Here Matteo di Giovanni abandons the language tied to the Sienese tradition of Domenico di Bartolo and Vecchietta, and reveals himself to be one of the most innovative painters in Siena at that time, infusing new life into the Gothic linearism of Simone Martini, as seen in the flowing lines of the Virgin's cloak.

DOMENICO BECCAFUMI (Siena 1486 - 1551)
**Annunciation Angel; Virgin Annunciate**
h. 128 cm; 126 cm, polychrome terracotta; inv. 3004, 3005

Created in 1545, these free-standing statues witness to Beccafumi's
extraordinary technical skill also in the art of sculpture.
The play of the draperies, the sweetness of the melancholy faces, and the
poses of the rounded, sinuous bodies immediately offer terms for
comparison with the eight bronze *Angels* Beccafumi made between 1547
and 1551 for the cathedral. The virtuoso modelling of the Virgin's cloak
over her head and shoulders recalls painted works by Beccafumi, showing
the artist's ease of handling both painting and sculpture, evident also in the
Annunciation angel.
Restoration carried out in preparation for the 1990 exhibition of
Beccafumi's work brought back to light the original polychrome surface,
although the Virgin's face still shows the flesh tones of a repainting in the
past.

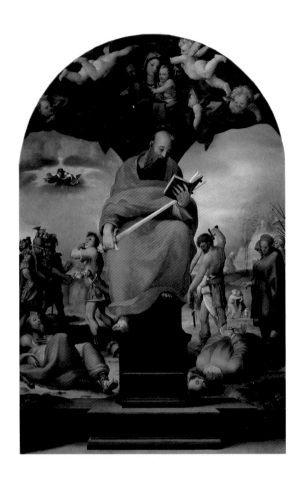

**D O M E N I C O   B E C C A F U M I**  (Siena 1486 - 1551)
**Saint Paul Enthroned**
230x150 cm, tempera and oil on panel; inv. 3006

One of the artist's earliest works, the panel was painted around 1515 for the
church of San Paolo, and after the church's destruction was transferred into
the Baptistery and from there into the museum.
At the center of the composition Saint Paul is seated on a throne set against
a pillar from which spring two large arches framing against the background
of a stormy sky the scenes of the saint's conversion (on the left) and
decapitation (on the right). At the top angels draw open a curtain revealing
the figures of the Virgin and Child and Saint Peter. The panel witnesses to
the artist's complex culture which creates an imaginative idiom, uniting
compositional freedom elements derived from Michelangelo with others
coming from the north (note the charming detail of the old woman and
children blown about by the wind in the right background).
Particularly dramatic are the chromatic contrasts of the green of the curtain
and the bright red and changing shades of turquoise of Saint Paul's clothing.

**L U C A   G I O R D A N O**   (Naples 1632 - 1705)
**Christ Before Pilate; Deposition**
195x139 cm (each), oil on canvas; inv. 3008, 3012

The paintings, both signed "Jordanus F," are thought to be works of the
artist's maturity, perhaps made when he was in Florence working on the
frescoes of the ceiling of the Medici Riccardi Palace (1682-1686).
The compositions, while still somewhat archaic in form, reveal innovative
aspects in the handling of the paint spread broadly on the canvas, and the
expressive vigor typical of the Baroque here begins to be placated.
The figures are more measured and sedate in their poses, and the search for
dramatic effects is not taken to extremes.
According to tradition, these two paintings, originally in the collection
of the Florentine Galleria degli Uffizi, were exchanged for the celebrated
*Annunciation* by Simone Martini, at the time in the church of
Sant'Ansano.

**G I R O L A M O   G E N G A**   (Urbino 1476 - 1551)
**Transfiguration of Christ**
415x375, oil on canvas; inv. 3013

This is the first XVIth century painting made for the cathedral. Created
around 1510, its purpose was to cover the new, larger organ installed the
year before.
Genga here is still under the influence of Luca Signorelli, with whom he

was working during this period (1509-1510) on the palace of the Magnifico Pandolfo Petrucci.

Christ in the center is flanked by two apostles while, below, three more apostles seated on the ground look ecstatically up at the figure of the Messiah. The grandiose, solemn figures are marked by their solid structure and full draperies, and a very human expression shines from their faces. All around them, interspersed among the clouds, swirls a crowd of lively, irreverent angels playing musical instruments and singing, rendered with special attention to plastic and dynamic values in the lifelike modelling of their limbs, delineated by strong, decisive contour lines. A particularly beautiful solution is the outlining of the solemn figure of Christ with the golden cherubs, whose flaming heads throw his solemn figure into even sharper relief.

# Sala degli Arazzi

Numerous documents reveal that determination was strong in Siena, starting in the XVth century, to establish a thriving silk industry in competition with nearby Florence.

The sacred vestments and hangings displayed in the museum (Hall of Tapestries) and conserved in the cathedral sacristy, originating in the Duomo and churches throughout the diocese, provide valuable documentation of Sienese textile production from the XVth to the XVIIIth century.

In the first display case in the center of the room is a rare and precious chasuble, attributed to early XIVth century artisans in Lucca. Against a beige background are embroidered parrots, palm fronds, ovals, and gazelles, while on the orphrey Annunciation angels alternate with suns and a pelican, symbol of Christ's sacrifice. The cases along the walls hold liturgical vestments, for the most part chasubles, arranged in chronological order. Beginning on the left nearest the door is the oldest Sienese piece in the collection, continuing with numerous specimens from the XVIIth century, with particular attention to the series bearing the Chigi-Della Rovere coat of arms. Also represented are examples of XVIIIth century and Rococo taste, with vertical ribbons and vine motifs and flowers and clusters of grapes. Special mention should be made of the chasuble in the next to last case on the right, donated by Queen Margherita of Savoy in 1908 to Venturi Gallerani, rector of the Opera della Metropolitana.

The richness of the materials, the cut and the colors of the vestments carry symbolic meaning, respecting a liturgical code connecting the vestments, especially with regard to color, to specific celebrations in the church year: white for the feasts of Christ and the Virgin; red for the Holy Spirit and the martyrs; purple for Lent and Advent; black for Good Friday and the Office of the Dead; pink for special holidays like the third Sunday of Advent and the fourth Sunday of Lent.

The entire room is lined with XVIIth century wall tapestries in flocked velvet woven in gold, originally in the convent of the Poor Clares in Campansi. On the back wall and on either side of the entrance are embroidered the arms of the Franciscan Tertiary Order. On the right wall, above the display cases, are recently restored canvases by Alessandro Franchi, representing the *Presentation of Mary in the Temple* and *The Nativity of Christ*, and by Luigi Mussini, with *The Coronation of the Virgin*. The two artists were part of the "Purist" school active in the second half of the XIXth century, represented also by the sculpture of the sleeping child by Giovanni Dupré also in this room. These paintings served as models for the decorations of the pinnacles of the cathedral facade, realized in mosaic by Venetian artists.

ROMAN MANUFACTURE  (second half of the XVIIth century)
**Altar frontal**
460x103 cm, satin; inv. 1137

The outer frame of this altar hanging is filled with a stylized flower and
tendril motif, while a smaller motif frames the five appliqued embroidery
panels. The side frames contain Saint Catherine (on the right) and Saint
Bernardine (on the left), separated from the central scene of the Assumption
of the Virgin surrounded by angels and clouds by two coats of arms of the
Chigi-Della Rovere family embroidered in gold and silk thread. An
interesting touch is the flesh tones of the figures painted onto the fabric
with tempera.

ITALIAN MANUFACTURE
(second half of the XVIth century)
**Chasuble**
120x90 cm, silk and copper gilt; inv. 1023

A tendril motif encloses the symbols of the four Evangelists and scenes from the Passion of Christ. On the orphrey, enclosed in medallions, are stories from the life of Christ alternating with figures of Saints John the Baptist, Mary Magdalene, Peter, and Paul. In the four corners of the frame enclosing the last scene at the bottom are the Chigi-Della Rovere and Borghese arms.

ITALIAN
MANUFACTURE
(XVth century textile; XVIth century
embroidery)
**Chasuble**
131x78 cm, velvet, brocade, boucle. Silk,
silver gilt, cotton, linen; inv. 1003

The chasuble, assembled using different pieces, is embroidered with a twisted trunk motif; growing from its center are small pomegranates in a polylobate frame decorated with leaves and flowers. The panels on the back (displayed here) are embroidered with scenes from the lives of Saints Abundius and Abundatius. On the front, on the orphrey is Christ Pantocrator between the Virgin Mary and Saint John, and around the neck are portrayed in polylobate frames two Fathers of the Church, Saints Peter and Paul, a martyred saint, and perhaps Saint Francis of Assisi.

GIOVANNI DUPRÉ  (Siena 1817 - Florence 1882)
**The Sleep of Innocence**
60x109 cm, marble; inv. 3602

The artist, the product of XIXth century academic culture, succeeded in balancing classical form with naturalism in a way that aroused the admiration of his contemporaries. In this work Dupré managed to give a realistic image of the child while working in the tradition of the nude recalling Tuscan Renaissance sculpture. The purity of the form is infused with a sentimental involvement worthy of the Romantic age, admirably achieved in the sweetness of the sleeping face and the attentive rendering of the details with a skill in handling marble that approaches virtuoso level. The statue was donated to the museum in 1953 by Laudomia Bichi Ruspoli Forteguerri.

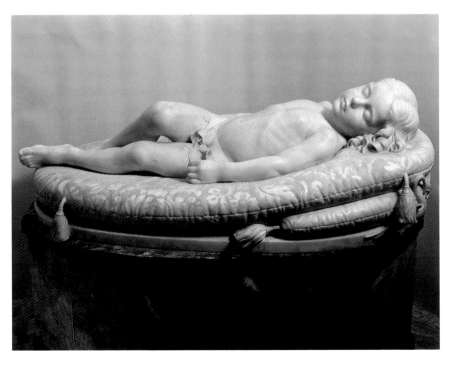

# Panorama from the "Facciatone"

In 1339, the decision was made to enlarge the Duomo with grandiose plans, for which the leading architects of the period were called to the city. Especially under the direction of Giovanni d'Agostino work went forward with great speed until in 1348 Siena was struck by the plague and the project had to be abandoned.

The structures erected to that point soon revealed their instability, seriously undermining the statics of the building. After numerous consultations, in 1357 the Twelve Governors of the republic decreed that the unstable structures be demolished. Thus the only parts left standing were the right nave (today housing the Museo dell'Opera della Metropolitana) and the superb brick facade of the new cathedral, also called the "Facciatone" (big facade). As one climbs to the top of the facade, above the doors leading to the loggia are two splendid bas relief lunettes by Giovanni d'Agostino, representing the *Virgin and Child* and the *Blessing Redeemer*. Giovanni's art recalls the painting of Simone Martini in the priority given to the rhythmic play of line, placing the sculptor squarely in the Gothic tradition.

From the top, an extraordinary panorama spreads before the visitor's eyes, showing Siena in all its splendor: churches, walls, palaces and towers, against the evocative backdrop of the hills surrounding the city. At the same time, one can imagine the vastness and magnificence of the new cathedral which the Sienese had planned for their beloved city.

# Sala del Tesoro

The Room of the Treasury contains examples of the goldsmith's and jeweler's art which for the most part came into the museum from the cathedral. Representing a panorama of the taste and styles which reigned in turn from the XIIIth to the early decades of the XXth century, pieces which stand out for importance and refined craftsmanship are the *Reliquary of the Head of Saint Galganus* (end of the XIIIth century), the *Chalice* signed by the Sienese Goro di Ser Neroccio (ca. 1430), and the *Reliquary of the Arm of Saint John the Baptist* (1465-1466). In the small adjoining room is displayed the precious set of objects used in the Chapel of Votive Offerings, built in the cathedral under the patronage of Pope Alexander VII (1659-1663) of the Chigi family; its very valuable pieces created in silver, enamel, gold, and rock crystal by Roman and French craftsmen in the middle of the XVIIth century, are true works of art because of the extreme refinement of the inlays and decorations and the technical

41

perfection with which they were realized. Among the numerous sculptures displayed in the cases along the wall opposite the entrance are especially noteworthy the very fine wooden *Crucifix* by Giovanni Pisano (ca. 1280), and the busts of three of the four patron saints of Siena (*Saint Savinus, Saint Crescentius, Saint Victor*), carved in the first decade of the XVth century by the Sienese Francesco di Valdambrino.

(Case 2)
FRANCESCO DI VALDAMBRINO
(Siena, ca. 1380 - before 1435)
**Saint Crescentius; Saint Savinus; Saint Victor**
h. 35 cm; 42 cm; 37.5 cm, carved polychrome wood; inv. 3191, 3192, 3193

Missing is the effigy of *Saint Ansanus*, lost in the first half of the XVIIIth century.
Brutally cut down to simple busts after 1776, the statues of the four patron saints of Siena were originally destined to the high altar of the cathedral, where they were to be displayed on the saints' feast day, November 18; each figure held in his hand a casket containing his relics. The delicate naturalism of the faces and the elegant, calligraphic handling of the hair declare openly that these works, of 1409, belong to the late Gothic tradition.

GIOVANNI PISANO  (Pisa, ca. 1245/1250 - Siena, before 1319)
**Christ on the Cross**
h. 110 cm, carved polychrome wood; inv. 3195

This *Crucifix* represents a moment in Giovanni Pisano's development anterior to the statues for the cathedral facade, probably around 1280, and should be read in the context of works – such as the *Crucifix* now in the Museo dell'Opera del Duomo in Pisa – considered by critics to belong to the artist's youth. The way the body moves through space is identical in both crucifixes, capturing the effect of total abandonment that follows immediately the moment of death. Typical of Giovanni Pisano's sculpture is the pathos emanating from the whole figure, marking by suffering even in the sensitive modelling of the spare anatomy.

(Case 3)
G O R O  D I  S E R  N E R O C C I O  (Siena 1387 - doc. until 1456)
**Chalice**
diam. 10 cm, copper gilt, champlevé and translucid enamels; inv. 3222

At the base of the shaft is the inscription: "+GORO/ DI S N/ EROC/ CIO. O/ RAFO." (Goro di S. Neroccio goldsmith)
The chalice, the property of the Archbishopric, was deposited in the museum along with its paten in 1924, and was shown in the Exhibition of Antique Sienese Art in 1904. The solid, elegant structure and sober decoration, without enamels, of the base give the chalice an austere aspect, significantly more modest than similar objects (such as the chalice in the Museo Nazionale del Bargello in Florence) assignable to Goro di Ser Neroccio's youth, suggesting a fairly late date (ca. 1430) for this piece, perhaps after his contribution to the Baptismal Font in Siena (1428-1431) and thus his contact with Jacopo della Quercia and Donatello.
Fully late Gothic in taste is the handling of the drapery in the enameled figures of the Virgin and Saint John on the nodule.

R O M A N  G O L D S M I T H  (XVth century)
**Monstrance**
57x21 cm, silver gilt, enamels, and precious stones; inv. 3286

According to Enzo Carli (1979), this monstrance was made in Rome in 1468, commissioned by Cardinal Francesco Todeschini Piccolomini, nephew of Pope Pius II. With the exception of the sunburst ornamentation, added in the XVIIth century, the object's formal characteristics fit fully into XVth century tradition, with a base whose outline is a sequence of straight and curved lines, a flattened ovoid nodule with raised diamond-shaped decorations, a hexagonal shaft topped by a sphere crossed by rows of tiny gold beads, all executed with meticulous attention to detail and inserted into a soberly elegant structure.

(Case 8)
ROMAN MANUFACTURE (first half of the XVIIIth century)
**Eucharistic exposition base**
32x4.2x20.8 cm, bronze gilt, wooden base covered with silver lamé;
inv. 3407

The origin of this object is unknown, but we do know that it became part
of the treasury kept in the cathedral sacristy between 1795 and 1798, that is
immediately following Napoleon's suppression of churches and monasteries.
The softly flowing forms and the sweet, rounded beauty of the figures places
the piece perfectly in line with artistic canons prevalent in Rome in the
early decades of the XVIIIth century.

(Case 9)
MIDDLE EASTERN MANUFACTURE
(XIIth-XIIIth century)
**Fragment of embroidered veil**
80x35 cm, linen gauze embroidered with silk and gold thread; inv. 3989

The veil was found inside the *Reliquary of the Arm of Saint John the Baptist* created by Francesco d'Antonio in 1465-1466 (see display case no. 14). It was a common custom in the Middle Ages to wrap the most venerated relics in precious fabrics, usually of Near Eastern origin. The repertory of decorative motifs (rhomboids, eight-pointed stars, and other geometric shapes, and pairs of facing peacocks separated by a stylized tree of life) on the ends of this very valuable fragment – a rare example of XIIIth century textile art – reveals an Oriental stylistic matrix, and more specifically, Arabic, for its origin.

(Case 10)
SIENESE PAINTER (FRANCESCO DI VANNUCCIO?) (Siena, doc. from 1356 to 1389)
**Saint Michael Archangel Enthroned**
38.7x27.5, tempera on panel; inv. 3405

The panel is the cover of a record book of the Opera del Duomo covering the years 1379 to 1405, dating the painting to 1379.
It represents Saint Michael the Archangel lifting his sword in sign of victory over the dragon. Although the painted surface is badly worn and abraded, it is still possible to appreciate in the better preserved sections the refined quality of the painting style and the solid placement of the figure in space; modelled with a soft, subtly shaded chiaroscuro, the image shows pronounced affinities with the work of the Sienese painter Francesco di Vannuccio.

(Case 13)
SIENESE GOLDSMITH
close to UGOLINO DI VIERI
**Crown of Saint Galganus**
circ. 71.3 cm, h. 11.8 cm, bronze gilt
and translucid enamels; inv. 3180

The crown was probably executed for the abbey of San Galgano, as seems to be suggested by the presence of the symbol of the abbey and the inscription "S GHALGANO DE CHIVSLINO." Like the *Reliquary of the Head of Saint Galganus* (see display case 15), the work most likely comes from the Sienese church of Santa Maria degli Angeli, where it was found in 1864. The refined elegance of the leafy scrolls forming the Gothic letters of the inscription and the technical perfection of the translucid enamel suggest a closeness in execution between this crown and some of the highest achievements of the goldsmith's art in Siena in the second quarter of the XIVth century like the *Reliquary of the Corporal Cloth* in Orvieto cathedral, created in 1338 by the Sienese Ugolino di Vieri.

(Case 14)
FRANCESCO D'ANTONIO (Siena, doc. from 1440 to 1480)
and assistants
**Reliquary of the Arm of Saint John the Baptist**
66.8x35.3x55.6 cm, silver gilt, translucid enamels, pearls, precious stones, and mother-of-pearl; inv. 3129

Saint John the Baptist's arm was donated to Siena Cathedral by Pope Pius II on 6 May 1464. Between 1465 and 1466 a series of payments are recorded by the Opera del Duomo to Francesco d'Antonio and "companions" for the realization of this reliquary which, within the sphere of Siena, expresses full adoption of the new Renaissance ideals. The *Stories from the Life of Saint John the Baptist* represented on it reveal clearly their debt to the style of some of the leading protagonists of the new season in art, such as Donatello, Domenico di Bartolo, and Matteo di Giovanni; the two pairs of angels holding cornucopias on either side of the windows of the reliquary case are an explicit citation of the classical motif of geni placed on the sides of ancient sarcophagi.

(Case 15)
SIENESE GOLDSMITH
(end of XIIIth century)
**Reliquary of the Head of Saint Galganus**
101x36.5, copper gilt, silver gilt, champlevé and translucid enamels, precious stones and colored glass; inv. 3128

Earlier in the Cistercian abbey of San Galgano, in the XVIth century the reliquary passed into the keeping of the convent of Santa Maria degli Angeli, where it remained until 1925. The date at the end of the XIIIth century (ca. 1290-1300) is suggested not only by a stylistic analysis (openly Western elements are combined with Byzantine influences) but also by the particular technique used for the execution of the work: the abundant use of filigree and the presence of champlevé enamels recall an archaic taste, still under the ascendant of the Romanesque.

(Case 17)
PAOLO DI GIOVANNI FEI (Siena, ca. 1340 - 1411)
**The Nursing Virgin**
75x50 cm, tempera on wood; inv. 3131

Earlier placed in the center of the Piccolomini altar in the cathedral, this sacred image was removed and transferred into the museum in the mid 1980s. The sinuous, elegant flow of the forms united with the painter's preference for lively, bright colors show his full adherence to the formal values of late Gothic art, evident especially in more complex works like the triptych of the *Birth of the Virgin* (Siena, Pinacoteca Nazionale, no. 216), painted in these same years (ca. 1390).

# Sala di Duccio

On the first floor, in a room with artificial light and constant temperature control, we find the supreme masterpiece of Sienese painting, the most elaborate complex in all of medieval art: Duccio di Buoninsegna's *Maestà* or *Virgin Enthroned in Majesty*. Painted for the high altar of the cathedral between 1308 and 1311, it was removed in 1506 after the decision to replace it with the bronze ciborium by Vecchietta, and dismantled in 1771. In its original location the *Maestà* was visible from both sides: on the side facing the congregation was the *Virgin Enthroned with the Child, Angels and Saints*, and on the back, facing the choir, were *Scenes from the Passion of Christ*; on both sides the predella panels and gables completed the iconographic program. Entering the room, immediately to the left of the door are assembled 25 panels from the back of the altarpiece, with scenes of the Passion. On the adjoining wall 19 panels which were part of the predellas and upper registers illustrate respectively *Stories of Christ after the Resurrection* and *Stories from the Life of the Virgin*.

Of the 9 panels that made up the back predella, the one that was probably first in the series (most likely a *Baptism of Christ*) has been lost, two are here in the museum: *The Temptation above the Temple* and *The Wedding Feast at Cana*, and the other six are scattered among foreign museums: *Temptation on the Mountain* (Frick Collection, New York), *The Calling of Peter and Andrew* (National Gallery of Art, Washington), *Christ and the Samaritan Woman at the Well* (Thyssen-Bornemisza Collection, Madrid), *Christ Healing the Blind Man* and the *Transfiguration* (National Gallery, London), and *The Resurrection of Lazarus* (Kimbell Art Museum, Fort Worth, Texas).

Dominating the room is the stupendous panel of the *Virgin and Child Enthroned with Saints and Angels*. On the right wall, two other masterworks contribute to the visitor's vision of the splendor of Sienese XIVth century art: Duccio's *Madonna of Crevole*, and the extraordinary *Birth of the Virgin* by Pietro Lorenzetti.

# Reconstruction of the front and back of the Maestà
(according to Curt Weigelt)

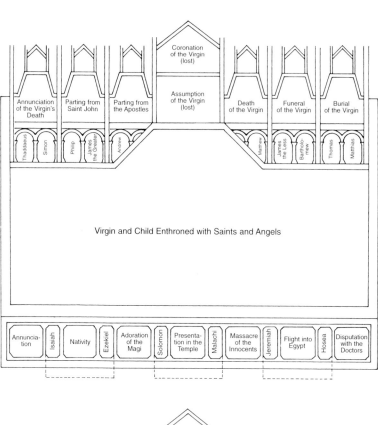

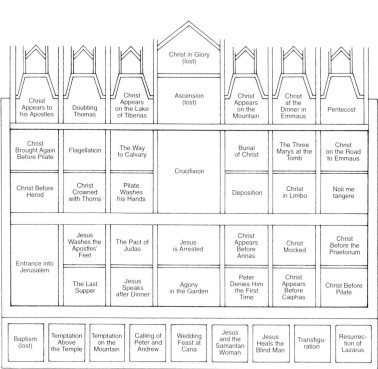

Back of the Maestà: *Stories of the Passion of Christ*

DUCCIO DI BUONINSEGNA  (Siena, ca. 1260 - 1318)
**Entrance into Jerusalem**
100x57 cm, tempera on wood; inv. 4501

The richly detailed scene is structured on various levels: the city in the background, the paved road crowded with people pouring out joyously to meet Christ, the bare, unadorned foreground.

The artist's realistic reconstruction of the architecture and landscape fuses with the figures to create a perfectly calibrated composition, giving the narrative a lively concreteness without superfluous drama.

According to the scholar Florens Deuchler, Duccio used as his literary source for this scene a Ist century text by Flavius Josephus entitled "De Bello Judaico."

### DUCCIO DI BUONINSEGNA
**Jesus is Arrested**
51x76 cm, tempera on wood; inv. 4504

This is one of the most crowded and agitated scenes in the entire cycle, showing here three distinct moments in the narrative: at the center Judas's kiss of betrayal, on the left Peter cutting off the ear of the high priest's servant, on the right the flight of the Apostles.
Even the landscape takes on a precise function in the setting: the rocks rising on the right accompany the flight of the Apostles who, frightened, run away from Christ, while the trees in the background create a circle enclosing the central scene and reinforcing the dramatic charge of the episode and all the scenes to follow, up to the Crucifixion.


### DUCCIO DI BUONINSEGNA
**Crucifixion**
100x76 cm, tempera on wood; inv. 4511

This is the largest scene in the cycle of the Passion and is marked by a dramatic intensity that here reaches its height. The representation plays on the contraposition of the two groups at the foot of the cross (as in Nicola Pisano's Pulpit in the Duomo of Siena): on the left the Pious Women and the Apostles, united in their suffering and as though frozen in dignified grief, on the right the agitated, disordered crowd of persecutors hurling insults at Christ on the cross, whose figure in the elegance and purity of its form recalls the refined modelling of Gothic ivories.

DUCCIO DI BUONINSEGNA
**The Wedding Feast at Cana**
43.5x46.5 cm, tempera on wood; inv. 4528

The wedding feast at Cana is presented by Duccio as though it were taking place in his day: the table settings, tablecloth, floor with tiles in a herringbone pattern, the wooden ceiling, decorative elements and every other descriptive detail are completely contemporary with the artist's life. The absence of the bride and groom, protagonists of the episode, contributes to concentrate the attention on the figure of Christ and the performance of his first miracle.

DUCCIO DI BUONINSEGNA
**The Flight into Egypt**
42.5x44 cm, tempera on wood; inv. 4534

Within the same scene are represented two episodes, on the left Joseph being warned in a dream, and on the right the Virgin and Child with Joseph fleeing into Egypt.
Particularly beautiful is the rendering of the landscape in the background, especially in the rocks on the right illuminated by the setting sun whose rosy light softens their harsh peaks.

DUCCIO DI BUONINSEGNA
**The Slaughter of the Innocents**
42.5x43.5 cm, tempera on wood; inv. 4536

Duccio imparts to the episode a predominantly moral value. Despite the manifestly animated grief of the woman on the left, the dramatic atmosphere seems as though toned down and somber, particularly in the representation of the two henchmen on the right who, with calm detachment and repeated gestures, are captured in the act of snuffing out young lives.

## Duccio di Buoninsegna
### Virgin and Child Enthroned with Saints and Angels
370x450 cm, tempera on wood; inv. 4538

The figure of the Virgin seated in the center on an elegant throne inlaid with colored marble dominates the composition of which she is absolute protagonist.

Surrounding the throne is a choir of angels, ten on each side, with in front of them the figures of Saint Catherine of Alexandria, Saint Paul and Saint John the Evangelist on the left, and Saint John the Baptist, Saint Peter, and Saint Agnes on the right. In the foregound kneel the four patron saints of Siena, Saint Ansanus and Saint Savinus on the left, and Saint Crescentius and Saint Victor on the right. Across the top, in aedicules whose frames have been lost, are painted the figures of the Apostles, with their abbreviated names written on the gold ground.

The visitor cannot help being dazzled by the splendor of the gold ground and the brilliance of the haloes and richly embroiderd clothes. Amidst this profusion of gold the artist uses warm, glowing colors, against which stands out the deep cobalt blue of the cloak of the Virgin, her magnificence enhanced by her larger size with respect to the other figures.

Astonishing effects of color and line are achieved in this symmetrically balanced composition, which shows influences from the aulic Byzantine tradition but at the same time Duccio's awareness of the new rhythms of Gothic art. Despite some rigidity of design, the soft modelling of the forms, the expressive force of some of the saints and angels around the throne, the flowing, harmonious line of the Virgin's cloak with the rippling effect of its gold border create in the viewer a sense of a heavenly vision, which would have been almost overwhelming in the altarpiece's original location on the high altar of the cathedral, lighted by candles in the dimness of the chancel behind the screen.

D U C C I O   D I   B U O N I N S E G N A
**Annunciation of the Death of the Virgin**
41.5x54 cm, tempera on wood; inv. 4521

The scene, set in a domestic interior, presents the angel who, handing a palm frond to the Virgin, announces her impending death.
The perspectival handling of the space is still somewhat uncertain (note the position of the chest on which the Virgin sits), but it nonetheless reflects the sense of peace and serenity with which the composition is imbued.
The lightness of the elegant figure of the angel, who has just landed in the room, is masterfully indicated by the sinuous swirl of the edge of his cloak over his shoulder.

# DUCCIO DI BUONINSEGNA
## Madonna of Crevole
89x60 cm, tempera on wood; inv. 4539

The panel, originally in the church of Santa Cecilia at Crevole in the Sienese countryside, was painted during the artist's youth, around 1283. The Virgin, portrayed half-length as was typical of Byzantine images, holds the Christ Child who stretches his hand out to touch her veil. While iconographic and stylistic elements, like the gold striations in her cloak and the red cap (*maphorion*) under her veil, recall Byzantine painting, the picture also reflects local influences and especially the innovations introduced in Florence by Cimabue. But the greatness of this work is evident above all in the sweetness of the ethereal, gentle faces and the effect of transparency in the Child's clothing, infusing the scene with the tender intimacy of the profound bond of affection between mother and child.

PIETRO LORENZETTI (Siena, ca. 1280 - 1348)
**The Birth of the Virgin**
185x184 cm, tempera on wood; inv. 4540

The panel, dated 1342 and signed: PETRUS LAURENTII DE
SENIS ME PINXIT A. MCCCXLII, was commissioned to Pietro
Lorenzetti in 1335 for the altar of Saint Savinus in the
Duomo, facing the altar of Saint Crescentius which
held the *Presentation in the Temple* by his brother
Ambrogio. This was the last work painted by the
artist, who died in the plague of 1348.
The painting was originally flanked by panels
with images of Saint Savinus and Saint
Bartholomew, and had a predella with
stories from the life of Saint Savinus and of
Christ.
Pietro's great invention consists in his
transformation of the traditional triptych
division into a new and modern
composition. Here the main scene and the
one in the section on the right are seen as
parts of the same space, with the pilaster of
the frame representing a pillar of the room
where the noble figure of Saint Anne lies
majestically on her bed in the centre of the
altarpiece, surrounded by young women
discreet and sedate in their movements.
The correspondence in perspective between
the squares of the tile floor and the arches
of the star-studded ceiling gives an effect of
depth which seems to prefigure Renaissance
inventions. The same can be said of the
scene on the left, where the wonderful
glimpse of Sienese architecture beyond
contributes to open up the scene behind
Saint Joachim, intent on the message
brought to him by the young boy.
Pietro here also gives us a valuable
document concerning the fashions in
clothing and interior decoration of the
time, with the rich fabrics used in the
furnishings of the bed and room.

# SALA DI JACOPO DELLA QUERCIA

The door to the right of Duccio's *Maestà* leads to a small vestibule lined with XVIth century wooden cupboards and *boiserie*; here are displayed wooden sculptures by Jacopo della Quercia and his workshop representing Saint Anthony Abbot, Saint Bartholomew, the Virgin and Child, Saint John the Baptist, and Saint Peter.

JACOPO DELLA QUERCIA
(Siena 1371/1374 - 1438)
and workshop
**Saint John the Baptist**
h. 96.3 cm, polychrome and gilded wood;
inv. 4604

The sculpture came into the museum from the church of San Giovanni Battista in Siena. The energetic, intricate drapery of his cloak and rippling curls of his tunic of animal skin find precise correspondents in similar motifs in the sculptor's *Saints* for the Trenta altar in Lucca (finished in 1422) and his *Prophets* for the Siena baptismal font (1428). This statue, which should be located chronologically between these two artistic undertakings, is assigned to the workshop of Jacopo della Quercia, who seems to be responsible for the design and a large part of the execution of the figure.

# SALA DEL CROCIFISSO

The Room of the Crucifix continues the display of Sienese wooden sculpture, uniting in a few square meters some of the highest achievements of the end of the XIVth and beginning of the XVth century. A XIVth century *Crucifix*, formerly in the cathedral sacristy, is flanked by *The Grieving Virgin and Saint John the Evangelist* by Domenico di Niccolò "dei Cori" (1414), and along the left wall are arranged *Saint Savinus Bishop* (ca. 1395) by Guido di Giovanni, *Saint John the Baptist* (1464) by Francesco di Giorgio Martini, and *Saint Nicholas* (ca. 1460) by Antonio Federighi.

FRANCESCO DI GIORGIO MARTINI (Siena 1439 - 1501)
**Saint John the Baptist**
h. 185 cm, polychrome wood; inv. 4622

The statue was carved in 1464 for the company of San Giovanni Battista della Morte, where it remained until 1784, when the company was suppressed. Within the sphere of Sienese sculpture of the second half of the XVth century, Francesco di Giorgio's *Saint John the Baptist* marks one of the highest achievements of Renaissance statuary, revealing a careful meditation and profound understanding of the formal principles underlying the art of Donatello (in the internal action of the figure and the pictorial treatment of the animal-skin tunic) and Pollaiolo (in the effect of movement suggested by the position of the legs).

DOMENICO DI NICCOLÒ "DEI CORI"
(Siena 1363 - 1450/1453)
**The Grieving Virgin and Saint John the Evangelist**
h. 169 cm; 168 cm, polychrome wood; inv. 4625, 4623

The two figures were commissioned from Domenico di Niccolò on 4 September 1414 by the Operaio ("head") del Duomo Messer Caterino di Corsino. The statues, finished in 1415, were placed in the chapel of Ser Galgano di Cerbone in the cathedral where they remained until 1676; after various transfers, they ended up in the church of San Pietro a Ovile in 1816. Here in the museum they are displayed in an ideal reconstruction of their original arrangement, flanking a XIVth century monumental *Crucifix* of the Sienese school.
Along with Jacopo della Quercia and Francesco di Valdambrino one of the leading sculptors in Siena during the late Gothic period, Domenico di Niccolò distinguishes himself from these two for his accentuated stylization of form, to which, as revealed by the faces of the Virgin and Saint John grimacing in pain, he unites a marked sensitivity to naturalistic detail.

ANTONIO FEDERIGHI (Siena, ca. 1423 - 1483)
**Saint Nicholas**
h. 193 cm, polychrome wood; inv. 4844

This polychrome wooden statue of Saint Nicholas was created by Antonio Federighi during the same years when he was working on the *Saints Ansanus, Victor, and Savinus* for the Loggia della Mercanzia (1458-1461). In the figure's proud stance the sculptor repeats the especially energetic and vigorous modelling seen in the marble statues of these saints.

## Sala dei Cartoni

The door out of the Duccio room on the left of the *Maestà* leads to another long, narrow room (Room of the Cartoons) whose walls are lined with scenes from the richly decorated marble floor of the Duomo. Along the left hand wall as one enters, scenes from Bible stories illustrated by Domenico Beccafumi are reproduced on copper sheets (XVIIIth century) while along the opposite wall are XIXth century cartoons prepared as part of a restoration campaign of the most badly worn sections of the floor. Immediately to the right of the door is hung a large pen-and-ink drawing by Giovanni Pacciarelli (1884) taken from photographs by Paolo Lombardi of the floor in its entirety.

Down the center of the room are glass cases displaying rare and precious illuminated graduals, antiphonaries, and psalters from the XIIIth to the XVth century. During the XIIIth century numerous artists worked on the decoration of the manuscripts; among these codexes, Antiphonary 33-5 is especially richly illustrated.

In the second half of the XIVth century the decision was made to prepare new choir books for the cathedral, and alongside Sienese painters like Sano di Pietro, northern miniaturists like Girolamo da Cremona and Liberale da Verona played an important role.

The choir books are divided into two categories: graduals and antiphonaries. The graduals were read from the steps (*gradus*) of the pulpit, hence their name, and contained sections of the Mass; the antiphonaries, descendants of the Antiphonarium Cento created by Pope Gregory the Great in the VIth century to collect the sacred hymns, contain the Divine Office.

At the end of the room is a bronze statue of *The Resurrected Christ* by Fulvio Signorini, cast in 1592 for the Piccolomini Library in the Duomo, which was placed on the high altar every year from the Sunday after Easter to the Feast of the Ascension.

The room is also of great interest architecturally, as here one can see surviving elements of the new cathedral: a Gothic window, the black and white stripes of the marble facing, and the sculpted figure of a prophet (1339-1348) above one of the side doors.

L I P P O   V A N N I   (Siena, doc. from 1344 to 1373);
S I E N E S E   M I N I A T U R I S T   (ca. 1420);
M A S T E R   O F   S A N T ' A N S A N O   (Siena, active from the fourth
to the sixth decade of the XVth century)
**Gradual 98.4**
49x33 cm, tempera on parchment; inv. 4651

The first five miniatures (1345) in this gradual represent one of the supreme
moments in the artistic development of Lippo Vanni. In the historiated initials
Lippo shows an ability to render space and volume unseen heretofore, which
indicates a direct contact with the workshop of the Lorenzetti brothers; the two
initials with the *Presentation in the Temple* and the *Birth of the Virgin* are precise
citations of the paintings of the same subjects realized by Ambrogio and Pietro
in 1342. The delicate shading of the chiaroscuro and the use of a thickly loaded
brush and mellow colors unite with a profound understanding of the manner
of Pietro Lorenzetti, toward whom Lippo turns now with increasing attention.
The other miniatures in the manuscript can be assigned to two different
artistic personalities working, respectively, around 1420 and around 1445.

## GALLERIA DELLE STATUE

The Sculpture Gallery houses some of the greatest masterpieces in the museum. Along the walls are statues of *Prophets* and *Sibyls* created by Giovani Pisano for the cathedral facade during the years when he was overseer of its construction (1284-1298). The iconographic program called for insertion into the facade of figures of Old Testament prophets and kings along with ancient Greek philosophers and sibyls, each holding a scroll with phrases foretelling the birth of Christ. The vertical thrust of the figures, enlivened by an impetuous spiral effect and wrapped in their drapery, and the intensely emotional expressions of their faces, with their features marked by deep shadows, constitute an epitome of the dynamism and vitality characteristic of Giovanni Pisano's sculpture. On the left-hand wall, set into aedicules, are half-figure busts of the *Virgin and Child between Prophets and Patriarchs* (ca. 1320?), originally placed around the rose window in the facade. These statues and a large part of the sculptural decoration of the facade and sides of the Cathedral were moved some time ago into the museum to prevent further deterioration caused by atmospheric agents, which in some cases have irremediably compromised their surfaces.

G I O V A N N I   P I S A N O   (Pisa, ca. 1245/1250 - Siena, before 1319)
**Moses**
h. 196 cm, marble; inv. 4689

One of the greatest and most significant figures in the Old Testament, Moses was chosen by God to lead his people out of their oppression in Egypt, and to him God entrusted the laws which the Jews were called to obey. The protuberances emanating from his head are a sculptural translation of the rays of light that according to Exodus 34:29 shone around Moses' face as he descended from Mount Sinai.

G I O V A N N I   P I S A N O
**Simeon**
h. 181 cm, marble; inv. 4705

Simeon, a "just and devout" man (Luke 2:25), welcomed the infant Jesus at the moment of his presentation in the Temple in Jerusalem, as the Holy Spirit had revealed to him that he would not die until he had seen the Christ. The grave intensity of the expression of his face is underlined by the tormented movement of his thick hair and flowing beard, divided into locks dug deep into the marble.

### GIOVANNI PISANO
**Miriam**
h. 181 cm, marble; inv. 4696

Moses' older sister appears here with the most important figures in the Old Testament because the Scriptures speak of her as a prophet. Together with her mother, Miriam managed to save the baby Moses from the massacre ordered by Pharaoh to eliminate all the Hebrew male children and is therefore considered a savior of the children of Israel.
The energetic spiral movement of her limbs, following the axis of her body in an upward movement, is as though blocked by the sudden twist of her beautifully modelled head.

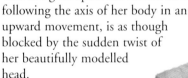

D O N A T O   D I   B E T T O   B A R D I called D O N A T E L L O
(Florence 1386? - 1466)
**Virgin and Child**, called **"The Virgin of Pardon"**
90x88x9 cm, inlaid marble; inv. 4751

Almost certainly this sacred image was originally over the ancient "Door of Pardon" on the right side of the cathedral very near the current side door; it was moved around 1660 when work began on Bernini's Chapel of Votive Offerings. Created by Donatello in the latest phase of his activity (ca. 1457), the relief represents the Virgin and Child with three cherubs, set inside a tondo whose perspective was carefully calculated – as can be seen in the foreshortening of the figures and the spatial rendering of the architecture above their heads – to be viewed from below. The Virgin's sweet, slightly melancholy face is very like that of Judith in Donatello's bronze group of *Judith and Holofernes* (Florence, Palazzo Vecchio). Beautifully naturalistic is the detail of the Child's hand creeping tenderly under his mother's veil to touch her neck. The rigid, schematic drawing of the cherubs in the background indicates the work of an assistant.

JACOPO DELLA QUERCIA (Siena 1371/1374 - 1438)
and workshop
**Virgin and Child with Saint Anthony and Cardinal Antonio Casini**
120x139 cm, marble; inv. 4622

The relief was made for the Casini altar in the chapel of Saint Sebastian in the cathedral, where it remained until the chapel was demolished in 1645. Considered by critics to be without doubt the work of Jacopo della Quercia, the relief, especially in the heavy, flowing folds of the drapery, show clear anaologies with the sculptor's late reliefs (ca.1437) for the portal of the Basilica of San Petronio in Bologna.

GIOVAN BATTISTA
SOZZINI (Siena 1525 - 1582)
**Elijah Fed by a Crow in the Desert**
91 cm (each side), inlaid marble;
inv. 4782

The inlay was part of the large hexagon
under the cathedral dome designed by
Domenico Beccafumi (1521/1524) and
realized by his pupil Giovan Battista
Sozzini (ca. 1562), who inherited his
master's drawings. As was the case with
many other sections of the floor, its
extremely consumed condition
suggested its substitution in 1878 with a
scene of the same subject realized by
Alessandro Franchi.

SIENESE CRAFTSMEN
(second half of XIVth century)
**Symbol of the City of Pisa**
diam. 72 cm, mosaic; inv. 5150

The tondo (ca. 1373) comes from the second frame, starting from the door,
in the central nave of the cathedral, representing *The Sienese She-Wolf with
the Twins Aschius and Senius surrounded by Symbols of its Allied Cities*
(Arezzo, Florence, Lucca, Pisa, Viterbo, Perugia, Rome, and Orvieto) to
symbolize the continuity of Siena with ancient Rome.

# Sala del Portone Centrale del Duomo

School of G I O V A N N I  P I S A N O
(Pisa, ca. 1245/1250 - Siena, before 1319)
**Two columns**
135, 278, 190, 200, 176, 234 cm (respectively), marble;
inv. 4781-4786

The marble fragments which are housed in the Room of
the Central Portal of the Cathedral belong to two
columns decorating the splays of the main door of the
Duomo. As indicated by the deeply carved surfaces and
the typically Gothic exuberance of the vegetable motif
from which burst out human and animal figures, the
columns were in all probability created between 1284
and 1296, when Giovanni Pisano was overseer of the
work on the cathedral; his was in fact the design of the
lower section of the facade, characterized by three wide
portals topped by triangular cusps.

# Sala degli Apostoli

The Room of the Apostles houses the statues of the *Twelve Apostles*
sculpted by Giovanni Pisano's workshop to decorate the cornices of the
central and right nave of the cathedral. It is not known when the statues
were actually realized; inspiration from Giovanni Pisano's art – clearly
evident in the expressive force of the figures – seems here to yield to a
more delicate modelling of the surfaces, in harmony with the style of
painting characteristic of Simone Martini's early work. The complicated
play of drapery and elegantly calligraphic line of the cloaks seems
inspired by similar motifs in the figures of saints frescoed by Simone on
the intrados of the entrance arch to the Saint Martin chapel in the
Lower Church of San Francesco in Assisi, whose date of 1317 gives us a
possible chronological reference for these *Apostles*.

# GIOVANNI D'AGOSTINO (Siena 1311 - ca. 1348)
## Christ the Judge adored by Two Angels
h. 140 cm (Christ); 122 cm (angels), marble; inv. 4807, 4808, 4809

The three statues were part of a sculpture group placed in the new cathedral in the 1340s, set in a lunette above the door in the eastern side of what would have been the right nave of the new church. Giovanni d'Agostino here gives an intelligent interpretation of the contemporary painting of Simone Martini (see in particular the complex articulation of the clothing and the refined design of the facial features) in an attempt to place sculpture in line with the elegance and refinement of the Gothic sensibility that found in Siena its supreme exponents in Simone Martini and the painters in his circle.

# Church of San Niccolò in Sasso

Originally annexed to the Spedaletto di Monna Agnese, a charitable institution founded by Monna Agnese di Orlando in the second half of the XIIIth century to assist needy mothers and girls, the church of San Niccolò is a rare example in Siena of a late Baroque interior with paintings from the same epoch. Between 1607 and 1612 the modest church then existing was enlarged and remodeled. Decoration of the interior lasted for a period of about twenty years and was enriched by canvases by the most important Sienese painters of the first half of the XVIIth century.

Above the high altar hangs a very fine altarpiece by Francesco Vanni, representing *The Virgin and Child Enthroned with Saints Lawrence, Gregory, Nicholas, and Agnes*, painted during the last period of the artist's life (he died in 1610). The serene, balanced composition is enlivened by the vibrant effects of the light that, pouring down on the figures, sets up a play of reflections and transparencies. Works by Rutilio Manetti and the artist's son Raffaello Vanni, his students, decorate the other altars in the church. Along with classical and baroque elements coming from Bologna and Rome, they reveal an interest in light effects inspired by the great example of Caravaggio whose solutions are adopted, for example, in Manetti's painting *The Resurrection of Christ* where the figure of the soldier on the left recalls the shouting boy in Caravaggio's *Martyrdom of Saint Matthew* in the church of San Luigi dei Francesi in Rome.

The elegant tomb slab in the center of the church floor (1613) is the work of Ascanio Covatti, who also designed the high altar. Above the altar is a gilded wood canopy with cherubs by Domenico Arrighetti and Giovan Battista Spampani and a Monogram of Christ carved by Master Giulio "*legnaiolo*" ("woodworker") and gilded by Cristofano Rustici.

The two gilded wooden statues of the *Annunciation Angel* and the *Virgin Annunciate* flanking the altar, as well as the statues near the front door of *Augustus* and a *Sibyl* and the rich stucco decoration of the interior (second-third decade of the XVIIth century) are the work of the well-known master Ludovico Chiappini. The scenes in the stucco frames on the ceiling, painted about twenty years later, represent the last phase in the decoration of the church and are the work of Gianbattista Giustammiani, called *Il Francesino* ("the little Frenchman"), active in Siena from 1608 to 1643. The cycle, dedicated to *Scenes from the Life of the Virgin*, includes also sibyls, saints, and sacred allegories, in an idealized, sentimental style well suited to the devotional needs of the community whom the church was decorated to serve.